OSCAR ARIAS

by Kelli Peduzzi
with assistance from Ronnie Cummins

Picture Credits

© Byron Augustin, D. Donne Bryant Stock — 11, 30; Bettmann — 18; Sharon Burris, © Gareth Stevens, Inc., 1990 — 33; Casa Presidencial, San José, Costa Rica — 6 (above), 13, 14, 32, 38, 39, 41, 47, 48, 49, 59; © Joe Cavanaugh, D. Donne Bryant Stock — 27; D. Donne Bryant Stock — 21; Gareth Stevens, Inc. — 20, 22, 26 (both), 34, 42, 51; © Max and Bea Hunn, D. Donne Bryant Stock — 28, 35, 37, 55; Robert Martin — cover; Reuters/Bettmann Newsphotos — 6 (below), 8 (both), 23, 56; Milton C. Toby © 1987, D. Donne Bryant Stock — 4; UPI/Bettmann — 7, 19, 20 (above), 25; UPI/Bettmann Newsphotos — 16, 24, 44.

A Gareth Stevens Children's Books edition

Edited, designed, and produced by
Gareth Stevens Children's Books
1555 North RiverCenter Drive, Suite 201
Milwaukee, Wisconsin 53212, USA

Library of Congress Cataloging-in-Publication Data

Peduzzi, Kelli.
    Oscar Arias / by Kelli Peduzzi and Ronnie Cummins.
       p. cm. — (People who have helped the world)
    Includes index.
    Summary: A biography of the Costa Rican president who won the 1987 Nobel Peace Prize for his successful efforts in promoting a peace plan for Central America.
    ISBN 0-8368-0102-4
    1. Arias Sánchez, Oscar—Juvenile literature. 2. Costa Rica—Politics and government—1986- —Juvenile literature. 3. Central America—Politics and government—1979- —Juvenile literature. 4. Central America—Foreign relations—1979- —Juvenile literature. 5. Statesmen—Costa Rica—Biography—Juvenile literature. 6. Presidents—Costa Rica—Biography—Juvenile literature. [1. Arias Sánchez, Oscar. 2. Presidents—Costa Rica. 3. Costa Rica—Politics and government—1986-] I. Cummins, Ronnie. II. Title. III. Series.
    F1548.23.A75P43 1990   972.8605'092—dc20
    [B]   [92]   90-39917

Series conceived by Helen Exley
Series editor: Amy Bauman
Editor: Barbara J. Behm
Editorial assistants: Scott Enk, Diane Laska, John D. Rateliff, Jennifer Thelen
Picture researcher: Daniel Helminak
Layout: Kristi Ludwig

OSCAR ARIAS

Peacemaker and leader among nations

by Kelli Peduzzi
with assistance from Ronnie Cummins

Gareth Stevens Children's Books
MILWAUKEE

Together at last

It was a humid August day in 1987 when the five presidents sat down together at the long wooden table in Esquipulas, Guatemala. They could hear the whir of the fans overhead and the murmur of their staffs clustered behind them, but they paid no attention to the noise or the heat. The five men had spent the past two days closed up in a hotel room together, arguing and bargaining. They had even eaten all their meals together, so intense was their discussion. Finally, the moment that nobody thought could ever come was here. The presidents were concentrating on signing the peace treaty in front of them.

The five presidents were relieved, yet worried. They were relieved because they had proved to the world that they could sit down together and agree to make peace. No one had thought they could because in each of their countries there had been bloody civil wars. Some of the conflicts had gone on for decades, helped by interference from the United States and the Soviet Union. The presidents were worried because agreeing to peace was not actually having peace. Time would tell if the five presidents would honor the peace treaty and work to uphold it.

There was one president who had faith that peace could be achieved. It was he who had brought the four other men together. For President Oscar Arias Sánchez of Costa Rica, the road to peace hadn't been easy. For Central America to survive, however, he had no other choice but to try. For the moment, at least, he was glad to have come this far.

Oscar Arias was from a wealthy, privileged, and well-educated family. No one, except perhaps Oscar Arias himself, had ever expected him to become a peacemaker and leader among nations. Arias had just become the youngest man ever to be elected president

"We have an obligation to face history with responsibility. If we fail because we lack the will to compromise, the people of Central America are not going to pardon us."
Oscar Arias, quoted in James LeMoyne's "Arias: Whom Can He Trust?" New York Times Magazine

Opposite: After receiving the Nobel Peace Prize, Oscar Arias became even more determined to work for peace.

5

From left to right, the presidents of Nicaragua, El Salvador, Guatemala, Honduras, and Costa Rica sign the Central American peace treaty in Esquipulas, Guatemala, in August 1987.

President Daniel Ortega Saavedra of Nicaragua.

of Costa Rica. His country, a small nation of only five million people, had no army. What's more, Costa Rica was surrounded by other nations caught up in violent civil wars. The leaders of these countries were hard-boiled men of conflict, not men of peace. It was a dramatic moment in history when Arias brought these men together to put aside their differences and work toward an agreement. Who were these other men, these four divided presidents, and what had Arias done to bring them together? The world wanted to know.

Daniel Ortega

At one end of that long, polished table sat a young man looking glum. The glossy black hair, mustache, and glasses left no doubt: this was Daniel Ortega Saavedra, president of Nicaragua. For him, the peace negotiations had been particularly difficult. Oscar Arias had confronted him in front of the other men. Was he really ready to talk peace, or was he just present to look good for the television cameras? Arias knew that the others were against Ortega. If he could get Ortega to show goodwill, perhaps the others would, too.

In 1979, Ortega had led a group of revolutionaries in overthrowing the government of Anastasio Somoza Debayle, a cruel dictator. Ortega and his group took power, calling themselves Sandinistas, after Augusto César Sandino, the leader of a previous revolution.

For the first eight years after the revolution, Ortega had been popular with the Nicaraguan people. He had helped free them from the terrible tyranny of Somoza. Their lives had improved, but lately the people were agitated. Ortega had stopped freedom of the press and suspended other constitutional rights. Many of the Nicaraguan people were growing concerned that the Soviet Union, which was supplying the Sandinistas with weapons, was influencing Ortega too much. They didn't want a communist system of government and neither did Nicaragua's neighbors. Nicaragua was also much poorer now. Ortega had spent so much money fighting the war against Somoza's army that there was almost nothing left to feed and house Nicaraguans.

The Somoza soldiers, who called themselves *contras,* or rebels, received help from the United States. The United States was supplying the contras with guns, food, money, and military training to help them throw Ortega out of power. The contras claimed that the Sandinistas had illegally taken power and that Nicaragua was not a legitimate democracy. Ortega was desperate to prove that this wasn't so. The meeting today was his last hope to bring peace to Nicaragua and to stop the violence and bloodshed in his country.

> *"In democratic systems, everything that is not prohibited is permitted, while in totalitarian systems, everything that is not permitted is prohibited. These two visions of the world do not easily coexist."*
>
> Oscar Arias, quoted in Seth Rolbein's Nobel Costa Rica

José Napoleón Duarte

Seated next to Ortega was José Napoleón Duarte, the president of El Salvador, whose ideas about running a government were just the opposite of what Ortega's were. In fact, Duarte was helping the contras himself. To see the two men in the same room together, much less for the same purpose, was astonishing to most people. How Oscar Arias had managed to convince Duarte to sit at the same table with Ortega was a mystery to everyone.

Oscar Arias had tried to convince the other leaders that all countries should stop helping the contras and that Nicaragua should be left alone to settle its affairs. Arias especially wanted to convince Duarte of this. Arias firmly believed that if Duarte concentrated only on his own country's problems, prosperity and peace would come to El Salvador as well as Nicaragua.

El Salvador had been embroiled in a bloody civil war for many years, and Arias knew that neither side

President José Napoleón Duarte of El Salvador.

7

Above: President Vinicio Cerezo Arévalo of Guatemala.

was winning. Although the United States sent millions of dollars of aid to El Salvador, the people held little hope that this would cause the government to give attention to the needs of the poor masses. Salvadorans feared and hated their government but could do little. Citizens who openly disagreed with the Salvadoran government risked being killed by "death squads." Thousands of people had disappeared this way.

To fight back, citizens organized themselves into a guerrilla force in the late 1970s. By the time of Arias' meeting, this rebel force had been battling the Salvadoran army for many years. Although the fighting was fierce, neither side had gained the upper hand.

If something were not done soon to salvage what was left of El Salvador's people and its countryside, there would not be much left to save. Arias warned Duarte that if his army kept on killing innocent people, no one would support him. No foreign companies would want to set up their factories in El Salvador. His people had to learn to get along with each other if their economy was to survive. This is what Duarte was hearing at this table.

Right: President José Azcona Hoyo of Honduras (right) converses with General H. Regalado Hernandez (left) in Tegucigalpa, Honduras.

8

Cerezo and Azcona

Next to Duarte were the presidents of Guatemala and Honduras, Vinicio Cerezo Arévalo and José Azcona Hoyo. The governments of Guatemala and Honduras were also fueling the fighting in their neighboring countries. Both were helping the Nicaraguan contras and the Salvadoran army by letting them set up refugee camps and supply lines inside their borders.

Cerezo and Azcona welcomed the chance to be at this table. To be seen negotiating for peace would improve their images, if not the lives of their people. For their countries were even poorer than El Salvador and Nicaragua. They, too, had received millions of dollars in foreign aid from the United States.

Honduras and Guatemala had other problems as well. The Honduran people were afraid of the fifteen thousand contra soldiers living in their country. They feared that the contras might try to take over. Arias tried to convince Azcona that peace between the contras and Sandinistas would also mean peace and safety for his country, too.

The government of Guatemala was also suspected of violating the human rights of its citizens. Death squads had been busy jailing people without trial and killing them outright if their political ideas differed from those of the government. Other countries were becoming disgusted with the way the Guatemalan government was treating its people.

Oscar Arias Sánchez

At the farthest end of that long table sat Oscar Arias of Costa Rica. Arias was in his shirt sleeves, his mouth set in a determined line. He was signing his name to an agreement titled the Esquipulas II Accord. It was a thin document, but its size masked its true importance. The newspapers were calling it "the Arias Peace Plan."

Despite the many governments around the world who believed that peace could never come to Central America, despite the bloody struggles for power, and despite skepticism and interference from both the United States and the Soviet Union, Oscar Arias had done it. Four war-torn nations were signing a peace treaty. They were ready at last to attempt to live together in harmony.

"Change must come about through the rule of law."
Oscar Arias, quoted in J. S. Fuerst's "More Than a Peacemaker,"Commonweal

"[We will] urgently carry out . . . the steps for national reconciliation which would allow for popular participation with full guarantees in authentic political processes of a democratic nature based on justice, freedom and democracy."
From the Esquipulas II peace treaty, signed in August 1987

9

Oscar Arias took pride in his achievement. He had managed to get the others to agree to his peace plan even though his own country, Costa Rica, did not have an army. He had convinced the others of the need for a peace treaty without having the threat of force to back him up if they did not comply. He had accomplished this on the idea of peace alone.

Arias had acted primarily out of a sense of impending disaster. Costa Rica was one of Central America's few democracies. With the wars going on around it, however, its safety was precarious. If there were peace in all of Central America, he reasoned, then Costa Rica would be in less danger. The rest of the world watched in amazement. How had he done it? Could the peace plan really work? Would people really lay down their guns? Would each side give up its desire for power and agree to have democratic elections? No one knew, but they did know that Arias had achieved a nearly impossible task just by getting them to agree to try.

A long road to peace

Arias knew that a long road lay ahead for real peace in Central America and that a peace plan was really only a beginning. The reasons for the wars were deeply embedded in the land itself. In most Central American countries, a very few rich landowners held most of the good farmland. Without land to farm, and no other jobs, the people were poor and starving. Yet their governments would not help them. Instead, their governments were controlled by the wealthy few who did not want to share their land. The people had no say in their own destinies.

Secondly, these Central American governments were backed by powerful military forces. Even the elected presidents had to answer to the army generals, who held most of the real power. The main reason for the rise of the military was because of Central America's peculiar geography. It is an isthmus, or land bridge, that divides the Atlantic and Pacific oceans and connects the continents of North and South America. Its strategic position has made it an important security zone for the United States. Thus, the United States has helped the military governments remain in power by sending them millions of dollars in aid each year.

These two conditions conspired to overwhelm the needs of ordinary Central Americans. Prospects for change in their lives were not bright. As they had found out, any effort they made to establish a more democratic system was quickly and firmly met with cruelty and repression. They had no choice but to resort to fighting for what they wanted.

Oscar Arias knew well the problems he was up against. Designing a peace plan to satisfy both those in power and the rebels had been no simple task. In fact, prospects still didn't look good for the plan to succeed. That was because it called for those in power to share the power. As a man who had grown up in a country without war, violence, or even an army, Arias had experienced firsthand what peace with democracy was. Peace was not just a dream for a man like Arias. It was a reality. He believed in the reality of peace far more than war, and he believed in it strongly enough to stand behind it.

"While it is true that in El Salvador, Guatemala, and Honduras military governments headed by generals have been replaced by civilians who were chosen through an electoral process of sorts, in all three countries the real political power remains with the military."
Fred B. Morris, in "What Can Central America Expect from the Bush Administration?" The Christian Century

A rich young boy
On September 13, 1941, Oscar Arias Sánchez was born in Heredia, Costa Rica, a small and prosperous city not far from the nation's capital, San José. He was the

A field worker picks ripe coffee beans by hand on a Costa Rican coffee plantation.

eldest of three children born to Lillian Sánchez and Juan Rafael Arias Trejos. Oscar's family was rich.

His father, Juan Rafael Arias Trejos, was the son of a well-known legislator and government minister. The family was well off and could afford to send Juan to college. After college, Juan Arias became head of the Costa Rican Central Bank, where two of his brothers also worked. Young Oscar used to enjoy looking at the Costa Rican money displayed on the wall of his home. It wasn't that he particularly loved money, but his father and uncles had officially signed the bills, known as *colones*.

Oscar's mother, Lillian, was from one of Costa Rica's most wealthy and respected coffee-growing families. Her father, Julio Sánchez Lepiz, had started out as a poor ox-cart driver. But he had carefully saved his money and gradually bought enough land to start a large coffee plantation. The success of the coffee plantation made the family into millionaires.

Oscar's future seemed safe and privileged. The well-kept mansions and lush parks in his neighborhood were quite removed from the strife present in neighboring countries. As Seth Rolbein points out in his book *Nobel Costa Rica*, everyone assumed that Oscar would grow up and help run the coffee plantation, make a lot of money, and enjoy a life of luxury and socializing with his rich friends.

A desire to be president

As a young boy, Oscar was sick with chronic asthma. This made breathing, and consequently sleeping, difficult. He couldn't go out and play as much as the other children did, so he liked to have his parents read stories to him. He especially loved the sound of his father's voice. As his father read, young Oscar dreamed of becoming an important man just like him.

One day, when Oscar was about six years old, his parents asked him, "What do you want to be when you grow up?" Without hesitating, Oscar replied, "President." Later Oscar would claim that he was destined to be president "since I was in my mother's womb," a claim that sounded boastful even to many of his friends. Not one of them thought Oscar would actually achieve his goal.

Opposite: Juan Rafael Arias Trejos holds his young son, Oscar, in their hometown of Heredia, Costa Rica.

A peaceful turning point

In 1948, when Oscar was only eight years old, Costa Rica experienced a brief but violent civil war that was to change his country forever. From this war emerged a leader who would have a profound effect on Costa Rican history. He would also have a direct influence on Oscar Arias' life. His name was José Figueres Ferrer.

In the civil war, Figueres led an army against Rafael Angel Calderón, then president of Costa Rica, and Teodoro Picado, the National Republican party's candidate to replace Calderón. Election results showed that the people had chosen another candidate, Otilio Ulate Blanco, as the country's next president. But Calderón and Picado refused to hand over power to the newly elected president. Seeing democracy in danger, Figueres raised an army and removed Calderón and Picado from power. Figueres then became temporary president, during which time he restored Costa Rica's constitution, set up democratic elections, and abolished the army forever. Ulate Blanco was installed as the rightfully elected president a year and a half later.

By getting rid of the army, Costa Rica had guaranteed that it could never wage war. This philosophy of peace

President Oscar Arias (left) stands proudly with his friend and mentor, José Figueres Ferrer (right). On December 1, 1986, the two men attended the ceremony celebrating the thirty-seventh anniversary of the abolition of the Costa Rican army.

was something of which every Costa Rican citizen was very proud. Everyone admired the remarkable thing Figueres had done, and he became a national hero. Although Oscar Arias was a child at the time, he was old enough to appreciate this formation of democracy and peace. It was an experience that Arias, the future president, would draw upon in his negotiations for peace with the four other Central American presidents.

Studious Oscar

By the time Oscar was fourteen, he had gotten into the habit of staying up late at night reading. The boy read everything he could find. Seth Rolbein points out in his book *Nobel Costa Rica* that Oscar was studious, not very talkative, and very serious. In fact, he seemed rather lonely and was shy and awkward around people. The self-discipline he learned from his private studies helped him when he began to attend the Catholic high school, Colegio Saint Francis in Moravia. There, in the high school yearbook, he announced that he was "studying to be president." Saint Francis gave him an excellent education, but it wasn't enough for Oscar.

At his parents' urging, he decided to attend college in the United States. His goal was to become a medical doctor. So Arias traveled to Boston, Massachusetts, and enrolled as a premed student at Boston University. He took courses in chemistry, botany, and zoology. He discovered, however, that he loved subjects like history and politics even more. Before he finished his second year in college, Arias had abandoned the idea of becoming a doctor and decided instead to study economics and political science full-time. His friends nicknamed him "El Presidente" because he still said he wanted to become president of Costa Rica.

The politician awakes

While in Boston, Arias watched the 1960 presidential race in the United States with interest. This race marked the first time that a debate between two United States presidential candidates had ever been televised. America watched in fascination as John F. Kennedy and Richard M. Nixon discussed the things they would do if they were elected president. The two candidates disagreed with each other on national television.

"It takes Oscar a long time to make up his mind sometimes, but when he does he's very single-minded."
A friend of Oscar Arias

Nixon's eyes shifted around nervously. He looked uncomfortable — not like a leader at all. Kennedy seemed poised and intelligent. He answered questions easily. It was the first time that most people had ever had the chance to compare two candidates side by side. People judged the men on their looks and personalities as well as on what they said. The fact that voters could see the handsome, smiling face of John F. Kennedy helped him win the election. Television had become an important force in American politics.

Kennedy the hero

The televised debate was a major turning point for the young Costa Rican, who sat glued to the television set. Arias was riveted by Kennedy's presence. According to Seth Rolbein, author of *Nobel Costa Rica*, Kennedy's sophisticated wit, intellect, and reserved good humor deeply impressed Arias. Kennedy's humanitarian outlook also made a deep impression on Arias. Even more important to Arias, Kennedy symbolized a new generation that was ready to assume leadership over

While studying in the United States, Oscar Arias began following the political career of John F. Kennedy. Kennedy, seen here in October 1963 with his wife, Jacqueline, and their children, Caroline and John, Jr., became Arias' hero.

the old, stale politicians of the past. When Arias ran for Costa Rica's presidency twenty-five years later, he would emulate Kennedy's style.

After Kennedy was elected, Arias decided to write a letter to him. It was actually more of a long essay, which he titled "This Is How I See It." The essay told Kennedy about what Central Americans were hoping for from the new leaders of the United States. To his great surprise and jubilation, Arias soon received an invitation to visit President Kennedy at his vacation home in Hyannis Port, Massachusetts. For Arias, it was the thrill of a lifetime to actually shake hands with his political hero. It was an event he would remark upon for many years to come.

Further study

Arias decided to return to Costa Rica to finish his education. He enrolled at the University of Costa Rica in San José, where he plunged into the study of Costa Rica's economic and legal systems. While he was at the university, Arias met José Figueres Ferrer, the leader who had abolished Costa Rica's army. Figueres was now the head of the National Liberation Party (PLN), a party he had founded in 1951. Arias became a member of the PLN and worked on national policies. The young man impressed Figueres very much. This is the sort of person who could go far, Figueres thought. In 1965, Arias became more involved with politics when he assisted a PLN candidate running for president. The candidate lost, but the experience had given Arias the itch to get into politics himself.

In 1967, Arias graduated from the university. He decided to go immediately on to further study in graduate school and received a scholarship to study at the University of Essex and the London School of Economics in England. Soon, Arias was on his way abroad again, ready to immerse himself in his studies. He was away from Costa Rica for two years.

One of the most important lessons that Arias learned in England was diplomacy, according to Seth Rolbein in *Nobel Costa Rica*. He learned how to debate, reason, negotiate, and compromise. The incredible civility of the English people also struck him. He observed that their courtesy helped them when trying to get two sides

Scenes such as this of Portobello Road, London, greeted Oscar Arias when he traveled to England during the 1960s to study at the London School of Economics.

to agree on something. The skills he learned in England served President Arias well when he was surrounded by four other presidents who disagreed deeply and sometimes violently on matters of government.

Nicaragua: in the shadow of the United States

Little did Arias realize that he would be a peacemaker during the most turbulent times in Central America's history. The odds against his success were huge. In Nicaragua, for instance, Arias was up against the country's long history of being invaded, colonized, conquered, or otherwise interfered with by other countries, especially Arias' strongest supporter, the United States.

In fact, for the past two hundred years, the United States has been deeply involved in Central American politics and economics. The United States has felt this involvement was necessary to protect itself from Communist influences so close to home. It has tried to keep any left-wing governments from taking power in Central America and shifting the region's power toward the Soviet Union.

As a result, the United States has often found itself supporting repressive — even violent — dictators and right-wing governments. These governments have helped protect the interests of the United States in Central America.

This was the case in Nicaragua in 1912. The United States Marine Corps was sent in to help the Nicaraguan Conservative party stage a revolt against President Jose Santos Zelaya. Once Zelaya had been removed from office, the marines occupied Nicaragua for most of the next twenty years. During that time, the United States controlled the Nicaraguan economy and set up its banking system.

"The General of Free Men"

To many Nicaraguans, it felt as if the United States controlled the Nicaraguan government. This made the citizens of Nicaragua very angry.

One person in particular, Augusto César Sandino, decided that the Yankee invaders were intolerable. He organized an army of peasants to fight the United States Marines and their Conservative party friends. The marines fought back, but Sandino's army had the support of most of the Nicaraguan people. The marines could not defeat Sandino and finally left in 1933 after a liberal president, Juan Bautista Sacasa, was elected. For his part in this, which many Nicaraguans considered a victory, Sandino's followers began calling him the "General of Free Men."

The Somoza dictators

Before the United States Marines left Nicaragua, however, they set up and trained a Nicaraguan National Guard. They also appointed an English-speaking Nicaraguan soldier named Anastasio Somoza García to run it. Somoza considered Sandino to be a troublemaker. One night, Somoza's guards ambushed Sandino and killed him. Their next target was President Juan Batista Sacasa, and they assassinated him, too.

Somoza then took power and ruled Nicaragua as a dictator. He was ruthless and cruel, but he had the United States government backing him. In 1956, Somoza was assassinated. His son, Luis Somoza Debayle, assumed his father's role. In 1967, when Luis died, his brother, Anastasio Somoza Debayle, took over. Nicaragua seemed hopelessly locked into a

"[Nicaragua] is an extraordinary threat to national security."
U.S. president Ronald Reagan

Augusto César Sandino, the "General of Free Men," led a successful peasant revolt against the United States Marines stationed in Nicaragua in 1933. Sandino was later assassinated by the guards of Anastasio Somoza García, who became dictator of Nicaragua after the marines fled.

Anastasio Somoza Debayle, the younger son of Anastasio Somoza García.

Nicaragua children walk past an archway that was bombed during the 1979 Sandinista Revolution.

family dictatorship, which held absolute power and absolute terror over the people.

The Sandinistas and the contras

But not all Nicaraguans had given up hope of recovering Nicaragua from the control of the Somoza dictatorship. In 1961, a group of citizens formed the Sandinista Front for National Liberation (FSLN), named for their original liberator, Augusto César Sandino. All of the FSLN's energy was devoted to trying to get rid of Somoza. During heavy fighting between the Sandinistas and the National Guard, Somoza fled Nicaragua on July 19, 1979. Members of his guard fled to neighboring Honduras, where they regrouped to form the rebel army known as the contras.

The Sandinistas got to work trying to establish law and order in a country that had been repressed by a violent ruler and torn by the revolution. In 1984, they organized democratic elections, and 80 percent of Nicaragua's eligible voters turned out. All political parties, even those of the conservative right wing that were sympathetic to Somoza, were invited to participate in the elections. The Conservative party, however, refused to participate. Its leaders demanded that the Sandinistas negotiate for power directly with the contras first. The Sandinistas refused. The contras were the

hated Somoza guards whom they had just chased out of Nicaragua. The Sandinistas would not agree to talk with them. If the Conservatives did not want to participate in the elections, said the Sandinistas, that was their business.

Without any opposition, the election was a landslide for the Sandinista party. Daniel Ortega was elected president, and two-thirds of the seats in the National Assembly were won by Sandinistas. Three other political parties shared most of the remaining seats in the assembly. A few seats went to communist candidates. It appeared that democracy had been established in Nicaragua.

United States aid to the contras

What the Sandinistas didn't know was that the United States Central Intelligence Agency (CIA), had secretly begun to help the contras who were hiding out in Honduras. The CIA trained the contras in guerrilla warfare. Guerrilla warfare consists of secret fighting tactics that rely on terrorism and ambush rather than direct combat.

The president of the United States at the time, Ronald Reagan, had begun to publicly demand military aid to the contras. He wanted to help the contras organize a counterrevolution and take back power from the Sandinistas. Reagan believed that the Sandinistas had rigged the election to give themselves all the power, even though there was evidence to the contrary. From 1981 to 1986, the United States government spent millions of dollars in aid to the contras. The contras used the money to launch missiles against Sandinista targets. A civil war was soon in full swing, Nicaraguan against Nicaraguan.

Why Arias wanted peace

Arias was caught in the middle of the United States and Nicaraguan conflict. Costa Rica depended heavily on aid from the United States, but Nicaragua was its nearest neighbor. Arias was afraid that his country would be forced to take sides and be dragged into the war. Costa Rica had no army and did not want to fight in any war, or be a part of any war. Its creed was peace. The only way that Nicaragua could find peace, Arias

Sandinistas protested U.S. aid to the contra rebels in this public wall mural depicting a Nicaraguan peasant wrapped in the American flag.

"[The contras] are part of the problem, not part of the solution."
Oscar Arias, quoted in James LeMoyne's "Arias: Whom Can He Trust?" New York Times

---

thought, was if the United States stopped supplying the contras and the Soviet Union stopped supplying the Sandinistas. Without outside help, the two sides would quickly run out of money to make war and have no choice but to reach a peaceful agreement.

The same thing could happen in El Salvador, Arias believed. The Soviet Union could stop supplying the guerrillas, and the United States could stop supporting the government. Arias concluded that all of the Central American countries had to refuse military aid from other countries and find a way to create democracy themselves. He was certain that this was the only way that Central America was going to find peace. This idea became the core of Arias' peace plan.

El Salvador: a repressive government

This Salvadoran neighborhood was built on top of a former garbage dump. Slums like these are a common sight in a country where the army rules. The people do not speak out against the poor living conditions for fear of being killed by a government death squad.

In El Salvador, Arias faced a similar struggle. The government of El Salvador was violently repressive. The repression had first begun in 1932 when a group of Pipil Indians and some communist revolutionaries led by Augustín Farabundo Martí protested a 50 percent cut in wages. The army was called out to stop the protest, and thirty thousand protesters were killed in what is now known as *la matanza,* the massacre.

Through the early 1900s, a small group of wealthy plantation owners controlled the government and all

the wealth in El Salvador. This group was known as the Catorce Familias, or the "Fourteen Families." The majority of the Salvadoran people lived in poverty. The people didn't get enough to eat or have decent homes. Conditions were so bad that 350,000 Salvadoran peasants moved to Honduras between 1961 and 1975, hoping to find jobs.

The peasants in El Salvador organized themselves into a guerrilla army in 1980. They called themselves the Farabundo Martí National Liberation Front (FMLN) after the early revolutionary leader. Their goal was to attack and weaken the government and its army. More rebel groups sprang up, some even organized by priests and nuns in the rural parishes. Other groups were organized by students, farmers, and factory workers. These groups protested the government's repressive actions. They demanded better wages, democratic elections, and an end to the killing of innocent people.

"In 1983, I directly discussed the very painful issue of the 'death squads' with [the Salvadoran president] and the Salvadoran generals. I explained that the United States could not, that we would not, be friends with governments that condoned the killing of political opponents. . . . Every murderous act they commit . . . alienates the people of my country."
U.S. vice president George Bush, quoted in Sara Miles and Bob Ostertag's "Absolute, Diabolical Terror," Mother Jones

The death squads emerge

The government retaliated against the peasant uprising. It formed *escuadrones de muerte*, or "death squads," that were responsible for crushing public protests. Their main job was to find and kill the leaders of the peasant organizations and the FMLN. Death squads also routinely opened fire on peaceful demonstrations.

A guerrilla guards a neighborhood that the Farabundo Martí National Liberation Front (FMLN) rebels have captured in San Salvador, the Salvadoran capital.

Salvadoran peasants are trained by the FMLN army. Some of the people do not even have guns. They must capture their weapons from slain government troops.

Those they didn't kill outright were kidnapped and never seen again. Thousands of Salvadorans disappeared in this way. Everyone feared being captured by a death squad, even women and children.

The threat of being killed or captured made the people even more determined to fight back. Eight thousand people joined the FMLN and began to wage guerrilla war against the government. The guerrilla movement was so large that the Salvadoran government grew worried. Without plenty of military help from the United States government, the Salvadoran government feared that the peasants would win and then establish a Communist government.

Government by terror

In an effort to make El Salvador seem less repressive, the ruling military generals picked José Napoleón Duarte to be president in 1979. Duarte was a moderate conservative member of the Christian Democratic party. He spoke publicly of helping the poor people of El Salvador, and the country's image improved. But in reality, Duarte was almost nothing more than a figurehead. The army let him carry out none of the reforms he proposed. It was content to let Duarte remain in office, however. He at least gave the

appearance that conditions in El Salvador were improving, and that meant that the United States would keep sending money.

Meanwhile, the FMLN wanted to hold peace talks with the government. It called for the government to respect human rights, share power with other political parties, and have an economy where the wealth wasn't concentrated in a few hands. The Salvadoran government steadfastly refused to talk to the guerrillas. Instead, it answered their pleas with more violence.

In 1980, a wave of terror hit El Salvador. The Catholic archbishop Oscar Romero was mysteriously killed after he had pleaded with United States President Jimmy Carter to stop helping the Salvadoran government. Shortly afterward, the death squads killed four United States nuns who were in El Salvador helping civil war refugees. When this happened, the United States temporarily stopped all aid to El Salvador and demanded that human rights be restored in the country. However, this did not last long. When President Ronald Reagan took office in 1981, he began sending aid again. The aid amounted to hundreds of millions of dollars, most of which went toward military funding and keeping the government in operation. Prospects for peace seemed utterly hopeless.

Archbishop Oscar Romero asked foreign countries to pressure El Salvador's government to stop killing its people. He was assassinated by a death squad in 1980.

"A truckload of powdered milk, rice, and meat tins donated by the Catholic church has been sitting in the garrison for seven weeks. . . . Soldiers restrict the flow of supplies . . . believing that the townspeople will give food and medicines to the guerrillas."
Janet Shenk, in *"Can the Guerrillas Win?"*
Mother Jones

Above: The political turmoil and death squad killings in Guatemala have orphaned thousands of children such as this little girl.

Guatemala: a nation of prisoners

In Guatemala, Arias faced more violence between peasants and the government. Guatemala's far-right government also used terror tactics and death squads to keep its peasant population under control. The government arrested students, professors, labor union and peasant organizers, and even church leaders. The death squads often drove through the cities during the day, snatching their victims, who were never seen again. If a victim's relatives protested, they were jailed and tortured.

In rural areas, young boys and men were forced to join military patrols and leave their farms behind. Their families were forced to live in refugee camps. The government promised them food if they cooperated, which, for most, seemed a better alternative than death.

Living conditions for Guatemalans were perhaps even worse than those in El Salvador. Thousands lived

Right: Many Guatemalan children, such as this boy, must work long, hot hours picking coffee and cotton or cutting sugarcane on the large plantations. Most families do not have enough farmland of their own and must work for wealthy plantation owners to survive.

Refugees receive care in a hastily set up camp in Quiche, Guatemala.

in cardboard shacks without any running water. Almost half the population of Guatemala didn't get enough to eat. Children begged or searched the dumps for food. Any peasant revolt, whether for land or better wages, threatened the ruling body's wealth, and thus its power. This was the reason for the brutal repression.

Despite their harsh living conditions, Guatemalans found energy to form resistance groups. These groups demanded freedom of expression and religion, equal rights for women and minority groups, freedom from repression, the redistribution of land and wealth to the poor, and the right to hold free elections.

In 1985, a report published by the British Parliamentary Human Rights Group estimated that 100,000 Guatemalans had been killed, 500,000 had been made homeless, and 100,000 children were orphaned by the violence. Despite this toll, the people refused to give up hope of someday electing their own leaders and being able to rule themselves peacefully. Their resistance continued even though it meant dying for their freedom.

Why, Arias asked himself, couldn't the United States give aid to the citizens of Central America

instead of to the violent governments? Why couldn't the United States help build democracies instead of obliterate "enemies"? With prosperous, stable democracies, Arias felt that real peace could come.

Honduras: the "banana" republic

Where Arias met no direct military challenge, he came face to face with the economic power of the United States over Central America. For the past eighty years, several powerful banana companies had controlled the railroads and produced 60 percent of the wealth in Honduras. These banana companies, owned by Americans, owned practically all the richest farmland in Honduras. This caused an acute shortage of farmland for the *campesinos*, or peasants, who then could not raise their own food. Many suffered from malnutrition. The Honduran peasants, and even the government, were controlled by the United States fruit companies. What the companies mainly cared about was profiting from the rich banana market. They did not want to give up a share of the land so that the peasants could farm it.

While the vast majority of Hondurans lived in poverty, the United States backed a series of dictators who supported the fruit growers. Honduras became another Central American nation to be used by its powerful neighbor to the north. Yet no serious rebel movement formed to oppose this. The few pockets of resistance, such as the factory workers who protested for higher wages, were simply ignored or silenced.

Strategic location

Honduras was in a peculiar situation. With Nicaragua on its southeastern border and El Salvador on its southwestern border, Honduras was right between two countries where the United States was involved in helping fight civil wars. If the peasants in Honduras were not helped somehow, they might try to stage a communist revolution of their own.

The United States wanted to make sure this didn't happen. The banana companies needed a cooperative labor force in order to make a profit. The United States government needed to keep Honduras stable so that it would have a good place from which to help the Nicaraguan contras and the Salvadoran government.

"In these thirty-nine years, thousands of Latin Americans have known exile, have suffered torture, imprisonment, and death at the hands of a dictator. In Costa Rica, no. Not one Costa Rican has left these lands and been unable to return freely. Nobody among us has known prison for expressing his ideas; not torture, much less death. . . . the minorities of one extreme or another, who believe that they possess the absolute truth, have never tried to dominate by force of arms. For us, liberty is a permanent fact of life, and respect of elections is a part of our national spirit."

Oscar Arias, quoted in Seth Rolbein's Nobel Costa Rica

Opposite: A laborer cuts ripe bananas by hand on a Costa Rican plantation.

This banana plantation is in Honduras. U.S.-owned companies hold most of the best farmland in this country.

So the United States helped establish democratic elections in Honduras. A civilian president was elected and a constitution drawn up. To cement its security, the United States gave Honduras hundreds of millions of dollars in aid to help its economy. Honduras became very dependent on this money.

"Yankees, go home!"

During the 1980s, resentment began to build in Honduras against the United States. Even the Honduran army, which had seen its power diminish because of the United States presence, was crying, "Yankees, go home!" Hondurans did not like the fact that their country was being used as a base for making war against neighboring countries. They wanted to control their own affairs.

In protest, four guerrilla groups sprang up in Honduras. They bombed U.S. military buildings and fired upon United States soldiers. They did not organize into a huge army, however. They stayed in small groups and chose not to mount a large-scale rebellion. They thought it would be more effective to try to educate the peasants and form labor unions. In this way, they hoped they could make a peaceful change.

The workers formed huge labor unions. By banding together, they could state their demands as a group to the company bosses. They could demand higher

"Let Central Americans decide the future of Central America. Leave the interpretation and implementation of our peace plan to us. Support the efforts for peace instead of the forces of war in our region. Send our people ploughshares instead of swords, pruning hooks instead of spears."

Oscar Arias, in his Nobel Peace Prize acceptance speech, quoted in Seth Rolbein's Nobel Costa Rica

wages, better working conditions, and the redistribution of farmland. If the bosses didn't agree, the workers could strike, or refuse to work until their demands were met. Some unions even demanded that the United States soldiers leave Honduras. Thousands of Honduran workers staged strikes that the government could not ignore. Labor unions became the main way of protesting in Honduras, unlike the other Central American nations. The government tolerated most of the protest, and thus avoided the terrible bloodshed of civil war.

> *"Every State has the sovereign and inalienable right to choose its economic system as well as its political, social, and cultural systems . . . without outside interference, coercion or threat"*
> From the United Nations Charter of Economic Rights

Costa Rica: a tradition of democracy

Oscar Arias grew up in a tradition of democracy. This background played a large part in his wanting to see peace come to Central America. Since 1821, when Costa Rica gained its independence from Spain, the country has been a stable democracy. It has elected all of its presidents, and, for the most part, those in power have obeyed the will of the voters. Except for José Figueres Ferrer's brief revolution in 1948, there have been no violent overthrows of the government or suspensions of the constitution.

According to Leonard Bird in his book *Costa Rica, the Unarmed Democracy*, the reason for democracy's success in Costa Rica has been the country's geographical isolation. The early Spanish colonists experienced this when they came to conquer the Indian tribes. In the days before roads and telephones, the mountainous land made communication, and therefore conquering, impossible. Without conquered slaves to work their plantations, the colonists simply became farmers themselves. Every family worked its own small farm. This tradition of equality influenced the way Costa Rican politics grew.

To help matters, a free public educational system was put into place, which allowed everyone to attend school. This meant that the general public was well educated and could participate on equal terms with the wealthy in the voting process.

> *"Costa Rica is the most democratic country in the hemisphere and we are friends of the United States, but we want a relationship of mutual respect."*
> Oscar Arias, quoted in James LeMoyne's "Arias: Whom Can He Trust?" New York Times Magazine

Difficulties

In the 1940s, the rapid population growth in Costa Rica resulted in a large housing shortage. Crowded living quarters without plumbing and water meant that diseases

Oscar Arias poses with his younger brother, Rodrigo. When Oscar became president, he named Rodrigo as his chief of staff.

spread more rapidly. There were not enough jobs to go around, and food became scarce. Costa Rica was not producing enough to meet the needs of its people, and the people were becoming angry and desperate.

At about the time that Arias was born in 1941, a group of citizens formed Costa Rica's Communist party. The party wanted to call attention to the plight of poor people. Party members organized strikes at the plantations where they worked. Costa Rica's wealthier citizens felt the workers were making too much of the problem. They pointed out that living conditions were much better than in any other Central American country.

To make matters worse, the Americas were drawn into World War II by 1942. To protect the Panama Canal, the only waterway that connects the Atlantic and Pacific oceans, the United States began to build the Pan-American Highway. The highway had to go through Costa Rica, and it was extremely expensive to build. Costa Rica had to borrow millions of dollars during this time. Another expense was the organization of an army, which had to be ready at any time to defend Costa Rica. The government sank deeply into debt.

The bungled election

Despite these difficulties and the protests of the wealthy elite, then president Rafael Angel Calderón was determined to improve life for ordinary Costa Ricans. He set up a social security system. He amended the constitution to include the Social Guarantees, a bill of rights for workers. He created a Labor Code that protected workers in disputes with their bosses. The conservatives thought that this was going too far. They accused Calderón of being a Communist. Even worse, they said, Calderón was the first president to have put their country in debt.

The situation worsened during the presidential election of 1948. Teodoro Picado, the National Republican party candidate chosen to replace Calderón, had been defeated at the polls by Otilio Ulate Blanco. Picado declared that the election had been rigged and said that it was invalid. He gave orders to have Ulate Blanco arrested and thrown into prison.

There was a storm of protest from the public. Out of this storm arose José Figueres Ferrer, a Costa Rican

Costa Rica's neighbors to the northwest include Nicaragua, Honduras, Guatemala, and El Salvador. Panama lies to its southeast.

who had been educated in the United States. He returned to Costa Rica to create a large *finca*, or ranch, near San José. Figueres believed deeply in the North American model of democracy. He believed that free enterprise and equal opportunity for all could coexist with justice. Figueres didn't particularly like Ulate Blanco's policies, but he absolutely detested Calderón and Picado's illegal manipulation of the election.

The surprise civil war

Figueres organized a small army on his finca, and he led it into fighting that lasted forty days. Because the government was so divided over the botched election, it didn't have the united strength to fight Figueres. Figueres' army secured a large number of guns, and it captured the airport. The government surrendered in April of 1948. Some two thousand people had died in the fighting.

Figueres had instigated and won the civil war. He declared himself interim president and head of a ruling *junta*, or revolutionary council. He promised that Ulate Blanco, the rightfully elected president, would be inaugurated in a year and a half. The opportunity for

Figueres to become an absolute dictator was there, but he did not take it. He had fought the war because he was a man of principle.

Figueres gave up his personal ambition and took the opportunity to make Costa Rican democracy secure. Very swiftly, he abolished the army that he had organized and made it illegal for Costa Rica ever to have an army in the future. He drew up a new constitution and gave women the right to vote. He gave the government ownership of the banks. With these decisive moves, Figueres had laid the foundation for Costa Rica to become a model of socialist democracy in a region torn by civil war and violent repression.

A peaceful existence

This, then, was the atmosphere in which Oscar Arias grew up. It was an atmosphere of peace, democracy, and compassion. When compared with Nicaragua, El Salvador, Guatemala, and Honduras, Costa Rica seemed like paradise. Although Costa Rica was not without problems, most people had jobs. There was enough to eat, and the government tried hard to provide enough houses for everyone. On top of this, literacy was high, and people were well educated.

Several different ethnic groups lived peacefully together. These included the descendants of five

A market in Heredia, Costa Rica, Oscar Arias' hometown. Arias worked hard to set up a cooperative system in which workers share both the labor and the profits. This provides a small country like Costa Rica with a wide variety of goods at a fair price.

Coffee plantations provide Costa Rica with a large crop to export to world markets.

native tribes of Indians; blacks who were descended from African slaves brought to Costa Rica from Jamaica; and descendants of the Spanish colonists, who had first begun arriving with Christopher Columbus on his fourth journey to the Americas in 1502. Many North American immigrants also moved to Costa Rica. All this diversity was packed into a total population of only two million people.

Then, as now, Costa Rica grew many important crops that it exported to other countries. These crops included coffee, cocoa beans, bananas, peppercorns, houseplants, coconuts, and citrus fruits. Unfortunately, the country could not produce everything it needed. So the United States began giving Costa Rica millions of dollars in aid every year. The government used this money to educate, feed, and provide medical care for its people. Not one penny of this money was spent on guns or soldiers, as was done in its neighboring countries. In some cases, the government had to borrow money from other countries to buy what it needed, so it had a large foreign debt. This caused some hard times for Costa Ricans and made them more dependent on aid from the United States.

"No army suddenly elevated Costa Rica's moral position to a dizzy height. If anyone tried to invade, there was no conceivable way they could argue that they were provoked. [Figueres] would place his trust in international courts and world opinion, much as a citizen places his trust in courts and the law of the land rather than resorting to his own rifle."

Seth Rolbein, in
Nobel Costa Rica

35

Arias returns home

In 1969, Arias left England and returned to his homeland. There, he continued his studies at the University of Costa Rica in San José. To earn his Ph.D. (doctor of philosophy) degree, he wrote a thesis titled "¿Quién Gobierna en Costa Rica?" ("Who Governs Costa Rica?"). The thesis was a history of political leadership. Through it, Arias was exploring the very roots of his country's democracy. Later, in 1974, this thesis would be published as a book.

But by this time, Arias had already been published. While teaching political science at the University of Costa Rica, he wrote a book called *Grupos de Presión en Costa Rica (Pressure Groups in Costa Rica)*. The book talked about democracy in action. The power of groups, not individuals, is what drives government, he said. He dedicated his book to José Figueres Ferrer, whose ideas had helped to inspire him. This book was published in 1970. Many people in the government read it, including Figueres, who praised Arias as a future Liberation party celebrity. The book won the Premio Nacional de Ensavo (National Essay Prize) in 1971.

Chosen by Figueres

Shortly after reading Arias' book, Figueres was elected president for a second term. (Costa Ricans may run for the office more than once, but they may not be president for two consecutive terms.) Figueres needed an economic adviser, and he thought the young professor would be perfect for the job. Arias was smart, but more than that, he had shown that his ideas were similar to Figueres'. Figueres also knew that Arias had helped a Liberation party (PLN) candidate run for president in 1965, which showed that he was loyal to the PLN.

Arias accepted the job. It was the opportunity he had long been waiting for, although the job was not very important or powerful. Arias mainly provided President Figueres with research about the economy, but he performed the job well. Because of that, Figueres promoted Arias to the position of minister of national planning and political economy in August 1972. Arias loved being the minister of planning. He traveled all over the country to find out which roads

needed improving or where schools were needed. Then Arias would decide which projects had priority, and he would direct them. During his travels, farmers and townspeople would talk to Arias and tell him what they needed from the government. This experience gave Arias close contact with the people of his country. Through it, he came to understand the people better.

While he was minister of planning, Arias also devoted himself to the construction of the Plaza de la Cultura in San José. Arias felt that this park in the middle of the city was one of his finest achievements. But it was certainly only one of many. Another was the large symposium, or scholarly discussion, that Arias organized to deal with the economic, social, and political development of Costa Rica. Experts from around the country came to talk at the symposium. Afterward, Arias gathered their reports into a book titled *Costa Rica in the Year 2000*. At this time, Arias was only in his early thirties, but already he was one of the most successful planning ministers in Costa Rica's history.

A supportive wife

In 1973, Arias married Margarita Penón Góngora. She was a beautiful, stylishly dressed woman with long black hair, big, dark eyes, and a friendly smile. Margarita was also intelligent and well educated. She had attended

The National Theater sits in the middle of the Plaza de la Cultura in downtown San José, Costa Rica. While Oscar Arias was minister of planning, he supervised the plaza's construction.

"There must be a fairer distribution of wealth, income, and opportunities. If our middle and upper classes persist in maintaining their present levels of consumption and property ownership, they will lose the social and political peace that they have enjoyed for so many years."

Oscar Arias, in
Costa Rica in the Year 2000

37

*Above: Oscar Arias'
wife, Margarita, provided
encouragement to her
husband during the 1986
presidential campaign.*

*Opposite: Oscar Arias
romps with his son, Oscar
Felipe, and his daughter,
Silvia Eugenia, before he
became president.*

Vassar College in Poughkeepsie, New York, where she studied biochemistry. Her family was very wealthy. The family had earned its money not from coffee, as Arias' had, but from a furniture business started by Margarita's grandfather.

Margarita's friends had tried to discourage her from marrying Oscar Arias, describing him as "that lunatic who wants to become president." She was interested in politics, too, so this argument did not convince her. Margarita and Oscar shared a passion for politics. People in both their families had held political offices. They were accustomed to the prestige and power that politics brings. It was only natural that Margarita would encourage her husband to pursue his lifelong goal of becoming president. She taught Oscar how to appear relaxed in public and coached him on getting along smoothly in social gatherings. Both of them knew, however, that actually getting elected would require a lot of hard work.

Up through the ranks

Arias now had support as well as ambition, and he plunged headlong into party politics. In 1975, when Arias still had two more years to serve as minister of planning, he was appointed international secretary of the Liberation party, the PLN. This post allowed him to get to know the most powerful figures in his political party. In 1978, he ran for the office of legislative deputy of Heredia, his home district, and won. This position was much like a United States congressional representative's job. Arias represented the people of Heredia in the National Assembly.

The very next year, Arias made his most crucial move. He decided he wanted to be secretary general — the leader — of the PLN. The powerful leaders of the PLN respected Arias, but they didn't take his ambition too seriously. He was so young, so quiet. He lacked charisma. Besides, they had been in power so long they took it for granted that they would remain there.

In July 1979, all the members of the PLN voted on who would hold offices within the party. The outcome was a surprise. Oscar Arias was elected secretary general by a wide margin. The older members of the party could not have been more surprised, including

José Figueres Ferrer, Arias' mentor. Here was a man just shy of his thirty-eighth birthday winning the leadership of one of the most influential political parties in the country.

In 1981, Arias helped the PLN presidential candidate, Luis Alberto Monge, run for office. Monge won. It was a victory both for him and for Arias, under whose leadership the party had won the election. Arias was becoming regarded as a powerful force in Costa Rican politics.

Arias for president

In 1983, Arias was reelected secretary general of the PLN, and his power in the party was secured. He took his reelection as a sign that Costa Rica was ready for a new generation of young leaders. (The majority of the population was under forty years old.) Recollections of the youthful and dynamic John F. Kennedy fueled his ambition to become president himself. The time seemed right. He announced to the other members of the PLN that he planned to run for president in 1986.

The news was not warmly received. His dear mentor, José Figueres Ferrer, wanted to run for president for a fourth time.

Privately, Arias thought that Figueres was too old and frail for a fourth term as president. Figueres argued that Arias was too young to be president at age forty-four (almost the same age at which John F. Kennedy had become president of the United States). Neither man would give in. Finally, Arias decided to go against the wishes of his old friend and try to become the PLN's presidential candidate on his own.

It was the most difficult decision Arias had ever made. In his own words, breaking with Figueres was "very tough." Then Figueres decided not to run after all. Instead, he backed another PLN member, Carlos Manuel Castillo, for the nomination. Arias was lucky, however. The PLN had recently changed the way that it chose its presidential candidates. Instead of a small group of powerful party leaders deciding who would be the candidate, any Costa Rican citizen who was a registered PLN member could vote for the candidate he or she wanted. Arias won the PLN nomination by fifty thousand votes.

Margarita Arias stands proudly next to her husband, the newly elected President Arias, during his inauguration in 1986.

The peace candidate

A terrible irony awaited Figueres. He did not want to back Arias for president because Arias had defied him. However, the candidate running against Arias was the son of Figueres' old archenemy, Rafael Angel Calderón. Calderón was the man who had helped Picado annul the 1948 election, the event which prompted Figueres to start the civil war. Figueres decided he had to support Arias' candidacy, if only to defeat the son of his enemy. "As long as there's a Calderón looking to be elected, he'll find me ready to oppose him," declared Figueres. Arias was grateful for the support, even if it was given reluctantly.

Arias started his presidential campaign with the motto "Growth with Justice." He talked about how the government would continue to run programs that helped people. His opponent, meanwhile, seemed inclined to revive the army. Calderón talked about how much he hated the Sandinistas in Nicaragua and how he agreed with Reagan's military policies. And Costa Ricans were listening.

Arias quickly changed strategies and began calling himself the "peace candidate." He promised to guard Costa Rica's democratic tradition. He said that peace could not be had through fighting war, but in avoiding war through peace agreements. This strategy worked. It reawakened the Costa Rican people's desire to

"A sincere heart, an intelligent mind, a firm and certain hand."
Lyrics from Arias' presidential campaign song, quoted in Seth Rolbein's Nobel Costa Rica

"Roofs, Jobs, and Peace."
Arias campaign slogan, 1984

A drawing by a Salvadoran child shows how peaceful village life was before the army destroyed the town's homes and fields.

preserve their country's neutrality. Everyone feared that the strife in other Central American countries would spread to Costa Rica if it took sides in the conflicts. Arias won the election and became president of his country. He had achieved his lifelong dream.

Caught in the middle

Arias had not campaigned as the peace candidate just to win votes. He meant to keep his promises. In his inaugural speech on May 8, 1986, Arias said, "We will keep Costa Rica out of the armed conflicts of Central America, and we will endeavor through diplomatic and political means to prevent Central American brothers from killing each other."

The danger of being pulled into the wars in El Salvador and Nicaragua had increased in the past year. President Monge, Arias' predecessor, had allowed the United States to set up security stations inside Costa Rica in order to monitor the fighting in El Salvador and Nicaragua. The United States kept guns and military supplies at these stations. U.S. officials kept pressing Costa Rica to help them get rid of the Sandinistas, promising more aid if Costa Rica did so. Contra

leaders had even moved to San José, where they openly organized war activities. Some Costa Rican citizens had protested the contras' presence. Theirs was a peaceful country, they insisted. A few of these protesters disappeared. The situation began to look ominously like that of countries with death-squad regimes.

The United States gave Costa Rica a great deal of financial aid. If Arias protested the United States military activity as he felt he should do, would the United States take the aid away? Without the aid, Costa Rica would not have enough money to build houses and run schools. The aid was also critically needed in a time when prices for consumer goods were rising, thousands of people were out of jobs, and the government was failing to repay the four billion dollars it had borrowed from foreign banks.

Arias believed that the wars in Central America were the cause of many of his country's problems. The neighboring wars frightened away investors from moving their companies to Costa Rica. The housing and job shortages were further strained by refugees flooding into Costa Rica from Nicaragua and El Salvador. Peace was necessary if his country was to survive. Losing the aid was a chance Arias would have to take if he were to preserve Costa Rica's neutral status and keep it out of war. Arias had to act quickly.

Arias proposes peace

Just two weeks after Oscar Arias took office, he met with the leaders of Nicaragua, Honduras, El Salvador, and Guatemala for the first time. Tension filled the room. Daniel Ortega was the only left-wing president there. José Napoleón Duarte, Vinicio Cerezo, and José Azcona were all right-wing. Arias was the only moderate. He believed in democracy, which made him different from all the other leaders.

Arias confronted the four presidents. Did they agree that peace was needed if Central America was to survive? Yes, they all agreed. They said, however, that their differences were so great that they didn't know how they could work them out to everyone's satisfaction. Arias pushed harder. Perhaps, he suggested, if the Central American countries tried to work out their own problems instead of turning to the

"I have always said that the worst enemy of democracy is cynicism and hypocrisy. I made a lot of pledges and commitments to Costa Rica, and in order to fulfill those commitments, we must maintain our peace."
Oscar Arias, quoted in Seth Rolbein's Nobel Costa Rica

"The most important virtue is patience. We all want to see things happen immediately, certainly in our administration; but many things just aren't possible to achieve quickly."
Oscar Arias, quoted in J. S. Fuerst's "What Can Arias Deliver?" Commonweal

United States or the Soviet Union for military support they would not need to make war. He pointed out that the United States and the Soviet Union didn't give this aid just for Central America's benefit. They had interests they wanted to protect, too.

This was true, the presidents agreed. Even though they called it "aid," the more powerful countries always wanted something in return for it. The presidents ended the meeting by deciding to establish a Central American parliament, where problems would be worked on only by Central Americans. Arias had taken the first step toward peace. He had made the others see that interference from other countries had only put them at the mercy of much richer and more powerful nations. If the Central American countries could solve their problems among themselves, they would be free.

Arias takes action

President Arias decided it was time that Costa Rica practice what it preached. He told the United States military advisers in Costa Rica that their forces would have to leave. He stopped the military training of the country's 8,500 police. He refused to allow any more contra leaders into Costa Rica, and he closed a contra military hospital in Costa Rica. The contras who were camping out near the Nicaraguan border were ordered

to leave. He even closed an airport in the jungle that the contras were using to move supplies into Nicaragua.

On September 24, 1986, Arias flew to New York City and spoke to the United Nations General Assembly. He said he would never permit Costa Rican soil to be used for military purposes of any kind, even if requested by "our best friends and allies in the international field." By "best friends," he meant the United States and all the foreign aid it sent to Costa Rica.

The reaction to Arias' deeds was swift. What he had feared now took place. The United States quickly cut its aid to Costa Rica by $46 million and withheld another $40 million that was due from the United States Agency for International Development. Without this crucial financial aid, Arias watched his country slip further into debt. Nicaraguan refugees poured into Costa Rica hoping to find relief from the poverty and war, only to discover their peaceful neighbor in dire straits of its own. Arias' advisers urged him to give in and help the contras so that the United States aid would return, but he refused. He would not compromise Costa Rican neutrality.

The peace plan

Arias had nothing more to lose. He had lost the aid, his people were suffering, and the wars continued. The time was right to put his ideas into words. On February 17, 1987, Arias called the four other presidents together again. At this meeting, which Nicaraguan president Daniel Ortega did not attend, Arias unveiled a proposal that contained steps toward peace.

First, all military aid from outside countries would have to stop. An immediate cease-fire in all the guerrilla wars would take place. Amnesty would be granted to all political prisoners regardless of their crimes or beliefs. Free elections would be held so that the people could decide for themselves whom they wanted in government. Human rights would be guaranteed, and military forces would be reduced.

Each country would set up a National Reconciliation Commission. These groups would settle disputes and work to make sure that human rights were not abused. International observers would come to Central America and monitor the elections to make sure they were fair.

"It is impossible to avoid the suspicion that Costa Rica's 'less favored nation treatment' is a form of revenge for having the temerity to disagree with [Reagan] about the contras."
Francis McNeil, former ambassador to Costa Rica, quoted in Martha Honey and Tony Avirgan's "Leaning on Arias," The Nation

"I told Mr. Reagan that I was sorry that while I had been able to convince Latin America and Europe of the need to seek a political approach in Central America, I had failed to convince him. I told him I would keep trying."
Oscar Arias, quoted in James LeMoyne's "Arias: Whom Can He Trust?" New York Times Magazine

Arias knew that what he was proposing meant big changes for the governments of Central America. One could easily compare his peace plan to the brave vision that José Figueres Ferrer had had when he abolished the army. Only this time, Arias was extending this peace to cover all the neighboring countries as well.

To achieve all the goals in his peace plan, Arias knew that the other countries would have to sacrifice millions of dollars in military aid from the United States and the Soviet Union. The repressive governments would have to give up power voluntarily and let the people elect their own representatives. The plan called for them to get nothing in return but the hope that thousands of their people would no longer die in violence and poverty. With this accomplished, he said, perhaps the aid would return — in a nonmilitary form. His peace plan called for sharing, compassion, trust, and goodwill among people. The plan was brilliant, and it was terrifying at the same time. The other presidents knew deep down, however, that the peace plan probably meant their countries' survival.

Doubts and hopes

Other governments and peoples all over the world reacted to the peace plan with both delight and skepticism. Within a month of the February meeting, even Ortega indicated that he was open to it. Almost everyone was thrilled that the Central American countries finally wanted to get down to the business of improving life for their people. What observers hadn't expected was for a plan to come out of Central America itself. The disagreements there were so deep that no one thought the countries could settle their own disputes.

In fact, no one was quite sure that the presidents of Honduras, Guatemala, Nicaragua, and El Salvador were sincere about peace. Some thought that they might only be unveiling this peace plan to make them appear like men of peace, when in fact they would continue to fight the wars. Some, like Reagan, called the peace plan "fatally flawed" because it called for all aid to the contras to cease. Arias insisted that the contras were never going to be able to achieve peace. They were part of the problem, he said, not part of the answer. In any event, Central America should at least

"The more Washington opposes Arias, the more prestige Arias gains."

Arturo Cruz, a former contra leader, quoted in Jill Smolowe's "Eyeing a Dialogue" in Time

be permitted to try to solve its own problems without outside interference, he argued.

Agreeing to disagree

In getting the four presidents to negotiate the peace plan, Arias achieved nothing short of a miracle. He combined boldness and intuition to get them to see that the well-being of the region as a whole was tied directly to how they ran their individual countries.

Arias had timed the peace plan very well. The United States Congress was just about to vote on sending more military aid to the contras. He hoped the peace plan would send a signal to the Congress that military aid to the region was now unwelcome. The economic crises gripping the five Central American countries was another factor motivating the presidents to agree to the peace plan. They didn't like all the things they were agreeing to, but their situations were becoming more desperate. They thought that by agreeing to peace, more economic aid would come from other countries.

Guatemala, El Salvador, and Honduras supported the contra war against the Sandinistas. But their leaders were willing to give up their support of the war if they could improve their public images. Perhaps foreign companies would want to settle in their countries

"Companies with operations in the region are intensely anticommunist, but there is a feeling that what Reagan is doing is not good for business, and that economic aid is what is needed down there."
    Gary Springer, analyst for Business International Corp., reacting to the CIA's mining of Nicaraguan harbors, quoted in Tom Barry and Deb Preusch's The Central America Fact Book

Left to right: Presidents Oscar Arias of Costa Rica, José Napoleón Duarte of El Salvador, Vinicio Cerezo of Guatemala, Jose Azcona of Honduras, and Daniel Ortega of Nicaragua greet reporters after signing the Esquipulas II peace treaty.

if they perceived Central America as a safe, democratic place to do business. For their part, the Sandinistas were willing to do whatever they had to do to stop funding the contras. The wars had cost each of the presidents dearly; each had reached a breaking point.

Arias knew all of this, and he had counted on their needs to outweigh their stubborn desires for power. At 4:00 A.M. on August 7, 1987, in Esquipulas, Guatemala, Oscar Arias graciously led Daniel Ortega, José Napoleón Duarte, Vinicio Cerezo, and José Azcona out of the hotel room where they had been working on the peace plan for two days. The five men sat down before a wall of reporters, television cameras, and microphones and signed the Esquipulas II Accords — or as it was better known, the Arias Peace Plan.

Back in Costa Rica, the people celebrated the signing by honking their car horns and ringing the church bells. For the time being, it looked as if war in their beloved country had become a remote possibility. They were relieved and grateful to their president.

Arias wins the Nobel Peace Prize

Two months after the signing, Oscar Arias had taken Margarita, and their children, Silvia and Oscar Felipe, on a vacation to a remote beach house where they could

Oscar Arias and his family return to San José after the announcement that Arias had won the Nobel Peace Prize for his efforts in Central America.

President Arias meets another famous Nobel Peace Prize winner, Mother Teresa of Calcutta, India.

relax undisturbed. While there, he received a phone call from his brother and chief of staff, Rodrigo Arias.

"They've given you the Nobel Peace Prize," shouted Rodrigo over the bad connection. Oscar was stunned.

"No, no, I don't believe it. They're probably just saying I'm being considered for it," Oscar said. "Oscar, I'm telling you, it's true!" shouted Rodrigo. Against all expectations, Oscar Arias had won the world's most prestigious award. He was only the fourth Central American in history to receive the peace prize.

Suddenly, Oscar Arias was the center of the whole world's attention. The Nobel Peace Prize gave him a respect and authority that other leaders could not ignore. The next person who managed to get through on the jammed phone lines was President Daniel Ortega. He congratulated Arias on winning. Arias wasted no time using his new advantage. He immediately asked Ortega to negotiate directly with the contras to lay down their weapons. Ortega agreed to try. In the past, he had always refused. It was another victory for Arias.

Beloved, famous, and influential

Arias immediately returned to San José with his family, and they were greeted with cheers and jubilation from

"The President of Costa Rica was hungry. . . . He hopped in his [car] and drove to a nearby corner restaurant. . . . Arias sat down, ordered a chicken taco and chatted with other clients and waiters — most of whom wanted to congratulate their President on winning the 1987 Nobel Peace Prize."

James LeMoyne, in "Arias: Whom Can He Trust?" New York Times Magazine

Opposite: Citizens of El Salvador parade through the streets of San Salvador chanting and singing for peace.

the people. People chanted "Oscar, Oscar!" in the National Theater and on the streets. Arias insisted that it was the people's award as much as his. Their country had been the model for peace.

Arias made plans to go to the award ceremonies in Oslo, Norway. Of course, he was taking his wife, daughter, and son. There was one more person he had to invite — José Figueres Ferrer, the father of Costa Rican democracy. The gesture meant a lot to Figueres, who was quite old by this time. The gesture helped heal the rift between the two men. Figueres was unable to travel to Oslo, but he was happy knowing that the peaceful journey he had begun long ago was a success.

Some people in the government and some of Arias' friends had always thought him too ambitious, even boastful. They could no longer accuse him of these faults, for he had achieved what he had always said he would do. And he had received the admiration of the world for his accomplishments. All of Arias' work had paid off. His quiet determination, thoughtfulness, and patient practicality had triumphed over violence. The Nobel Peace Prize proved that violence did not work and that nonmilitary action was the only solution to Central America's problems.

First steps toward peace

In his Nobel Prize acceptance speech in December 1987, Arias said, "Peace has not yet happened. It is about to happen." He foresaw the many hurdles facing him and the other presidents, and most of them became realities. The first steps toward peace looked promising, however. Each country had agreed, under the terms of the peace plan, to lift their states of emergency so that people could move about freely again. The countries vowed to restore freedom of the press, radio, and television. Most important, they promised to allow freedom of association. People would be able to hold political demonstrations without fear of punishment by the government. Finally, the countries promised to hold free elections. The elections would be monitored by international observers to make sure they were fair.

There was one major flaw in the peace plan, however. This flaw was universally recognized by all involved, including Arias himself. The flaw was that there were

no penalties in the peace plan for any countries that did not comply with its terms. Democracy would have to come about purely by the goodwill of the governments. No one would enforce the peace plan. Arias had placed a very risky bet on democracy. He had bet that the governments in power would willingly share their power with opposing groups and do it without resorting to more fighting.

Many people were skeptical of this part of the plan. When asked what he would do if one of the presidents did not obey the peace treaty, Arias replied that he would ask other countries not to trade with the treaty-breaker. Arias was asked if the threat of being cut off from money-making trade would be enough to prevent the treaty from being broken. He replied firmly that he did not support the use of military force for any reason. As a ruler without an army to back him, Arias had no choice but to appeal to the goodness of those with whom he was dealing.

Arias maintained that even if the peace plan failed, it would still have brought Central American countries closer together for the same goal. It would have helped create unity in a region so long torn apart. It would have helped build a sense of interdependence and community. That, he hoped, would be the least the peace plan would do in fostering a sense of self-determination for the five countries.

The peace plan in danger

The month after Arias received the Nobel Prize, Ortega was as good as his word. He agreed to negotiate a cease-fire with the contras, with the help of the Catholic bishop Miguel Obando y Bravo. Arias was overjoyed. The fighting would stop. Then perhaps the two sides could somehow work out an agreement to form a new, democratic government. Ortega also lifted the censorship of *La Prensa*, a newspaper run by a woman named Violeta Chamorro. He released almost 1,000 political prisoners from jail and freed over 1,800 former Somoza guards.

The joy was short-lived. Pressed by the United States and Arias to go farther, Ortega said he would never, ever agree to share power with the contras. The cease-fire talks fell apart, and each side vowed to enlarge their armies and continue fighting. In the United States, President Reagan tried to push Congress to send the contras $100 million in new military aid. Congress refused, saying it did not want to interfere with the peace plan. Ortega then cracked down on the free press, arrested people who opposed him, and behaved like the repressive dictator he had once helped to overthrow.

More conflict

Meanwhile, Azcona of Honduras and Cerezo of Guatemala had no success at convincing the army generals in their countries to abide by the peace plan. Honduras, in particular, was worried about the fifteen thousand contras living there. The contras were disrupting the countryside with their attacks against Sandinistas on the Honduras-Nicaragua border. If the contras' funding from the United States were cut off, as the peace plan called for, how would Honduras feed, clothe, and house the rebels?

The situation in El Salvador was, if anything, worse since the signing of the Arias peace plan. The left-wing guerrillas had asked to participate in the elections that were going to be held in 1989. They wanted their own candidates to run along with the government's candidates. Duarte was willing to allow this. However, his army generals, who held all the real power, refused. They said that if the guerrillas ran for office, the guerrillas were sure to win.

It was clear that the military powers in El Salvador would not relinquish their iron grip on the population or honor human rights. The guerrillas were furious. Their attempt to bring democracy to their country, instead of more fighting, had been rebuffed. They stepped up their fighting in retaliation. The government answered with more death squad killings. It was back to the old, brutal business as usual.

On top of this, José Duarte's health was failing, too. He had terminal stomach cancer and had to spend most of his time away from governing. Many Salvadorans and other Central Americans were worried that after the moderate Duarte died, a far-right-wing candidate would be elected to replace him. If that happened, the war might never end.

"So far, there has been an overall advance. The Central American governments still have disagreements, and sometimes we make statements that make it sound as if the whole agreement is going down the drain. But the desire for peace once again wins out."
Former Nicaraguan president Daniel Ortega, quoted in Time

A breakthrough

Arias and the world watched with dismay as the peace process seemed to reel backward instead of moving forward. The five presidents met again in February 1988 to discuss matters. The news was not good. The countries had moved very little toward peace as put forth in the plan. Arias gave Ortega and the others a lecture on the meaning of democracy. He insisted that Central Americans be allowed to vote for representatives of their own choosing. The wars had to stop.

Ortega responded unexpectedly. He announced that open, democratic elections would be held in Nicaragua and that all political parties would be invited to enter candidates of their own choosing. To give the other parties a chance to get organized, he said the elections would be held in one year, in February 1990. The other four presidents reacted favorably to Ortega's plan. Together they worked out a way in which the contra army could be disbanded and integrated back into Nicaraguan society after the elections.

Central Americans were jubilant once again. It looked as if democracy would take hold at least in Nicaragua. The United States Congress voted to send the five countries $2 billion in nonmilitary aid to help them rebuild their economies. The new U.S. president, George Bush, recognized Nicaragua's right to self-determined government. He praised the five presidents for their efforts and promised to support the Esquipulas II accords. This was something Bush's predecessor, Ronald Reagan, had always refused to do.

Elections in Costa Rica

Meanwhile, Arias was home in Costa Rica trying to stabilize his country's weak economy. He established a cooperative system, where people shared the labor, the costs of producing goods, and the profits from what they sold. He took pride in the fact that this gave Costa Rica one of the largest profit-making cooperative systems in the world.

But Arias' term as president was nearly over. The 1990 election loomed before his country. Forbidden by the constitution from seeking a second consecutive term in office, Arias knew he would have to step aside and let the new president carry on what he had started.

A street scene captures downtown San José, Costa Rica, near the Gran Hotel de Costa Rica and the National Theater.

On February 4, 1990, none other than Rafael Calderón, Jr., the son of Figueres' enemy, was elected president of Costa Rica. The people ignored the fact that Calderón was the son of the man who had catapulted their country into civil war. They also discounted the fact that he was the godson of Anastasio Somoza García, the former dictator of Nicaragua. Although Costa Ricans loved Arias, they noted that his party, the PLN, had won five of the last six elections. The people feared that the PLN was becoming too powerful. The scales tipped in Calderón's favor, even though he was very critical of Arias' peace plan.

Arias watched the elections with uncertainty and unease. Calderón approved of the United States' financing of the contras, something which Arias had strictly forbidden in his peace plan. Calderón had criticized Arias for "political amateurism," as though Arias had not known what he was doing. Calderón had gone further to say that to trust the Sandinistas to obey the peace plan was "a deformation of masculine values that was impugning the national virility." In other words, he was all but calling Arias a weakling. Arias

"[Arias] enjoys a popularity rating usually reserved for saints."
Lindsey Gruson, in "Costa Rica Elects New Leader Today," New York Times

Presidential candidate Violeta Chamorro flashes the victory sign as she campaigns in the streets of Managua, Nicaragua. She won the presidential election in February 1990.

hoped that the future of his peace plan would not be endangered by the aggressive Calderón.

Elections in Nicaragua

Two weeks after Costa Rica's election, Ortega kept his promise, and democratic elections were held in Nicaragua on February 26, 1990. An international group of seven hundred observers, headed by former United States president Jimmy Carter, monitored the election and declared that it was fair, free, and legal. The winner was Violeta Chamorro, former head of *La Prensa*, the newspaper that Ortega had once closed down. Chamorro had led the Nicaraguan Opposition Union (UNO), a group of political parties that banded together to defeat the Sandinistas. Amazingly, Ortega promised to abide by the election results. He quietly stepped down after years of the Sandinistas being the only party in power.

Nicaraguans and the whole world rejoiced. Arias' peace plan had won over violent war! Democracy had been established in Nicaragua, despite the contra rebels, not because of them. Almost 90 percent of Nicaragua's eligible voters had turned out at the polls. Some had even walked for hours over rough country roads to be able to exercise their democratic rights for the first time. It was an emotional moment for all Nicaraguans.

Now there was no more need for war between the contras and Sandinistas. All that remained was for the contras to agree to lay down their guns and move back into Nicaragua as full, free members of society, and for the Sandinista army to cut back its fighting forces. The fighting would finally stop.

On April 19, 1990, just days before President-Elect Chamorro took office, the contras and Sandinistas agreed to a cease-fire. "It represents a triumph for the Nicaraguan people," said Humberto Ortega, Daniel's brother, who was head of the army. After Chamorro took office, she sought Arias' advice about how to handle the contras. She and her advisers drew up a plan to give the contras complete amnesty, destroy any guns that they gave up, and reduce the size of the Sandinista army as soon as possible. Peace had come to Nicaragua at last.

A region still troubled

Since 1979, more than 150,000 people have died in Central America. The fighting continues in El Salvador, where the government goes on with its ruthless repression. José Duarte's death, which came right at the time of the elections in Nicaragua and Costa Rica, resulted in a lopsided and undemocratic election from which the guerrillas were excluded. A far-right-wing candidate, Alfredo Cristiani, was elected the new president of El Salvador. Despite claims that the election was both fair and democratic, human rights abuses still continue in El Salvador, and the United States government continues to send military aid from the United States. It is in El Salvador that Arias' peace plan has yet to fulfill its most urgent mission.

Good-bye, President Arias

On May 8, 1990, President Oscar Arias said farewell to Casa Presidencial, the home where he had lived for four years, and entered private life. Seeing him off were the presidents of El Salvador, Guatemala, Honduras, Nicaragua, Panama, and Belize. A large farewell dinner party brought them all together. The

"We have shown the world an example of civic duty, demonstrating that we Nicaraguans want to live in democracy, want to live in peace and, above all, that we want to live in liberty."
Nicaraguan president
Violeta Chamorro, quoted in
the New York Times

"Arias gave the eulogy at Duarte's funeral at 4 p.m. on the 25th while the balloting in Nicaragua was still going on. What he said was very prophetic and very eloquent. He said that Cristiani was the fifth democratically elected president in Central America [since the peace plan] and if the trend continues, Central America will be a different place."
U.S. Senator Richard Lugar,
MacNeil-Lehrer News Hour

"And even if everything were to turn out exactly the opposite of what I imagine, no malice could ever obscure the glory of having kindled this great endeavor."
Oscar Arias' favorite passage from Miguel de Cervantes' Don Quixote

other presidents drank a toast to their friend and peacemaker and wished him luck. They thanked him for helping to bring peace to their countries.

It was an emotional moment for Arias. Although he was only forty-eight years old, he had accomplished more than most people do in an entire lifetime. As he looked around the room, he saw that only one other of the original peace plan signers, Vinicio Cerezo of Guatemala, was still in office. All the rest had been replaced with leaders chosen in democratic elections.

Arias paused to consider the importance of this fact. Central America, he said, was on an irreversible path toward peace. He stated that democracy must succeed if 28 million Central Americans were to keep on believing in it. He also said that unless the Central American democracies work toward peace, freedom, and prosperity, they cannot survive. "That is the challenge for my colleagues in the years ahead," said Arias. With that, the peacemaker ended his presidency, promising to work for democracy and peace always.

For More Information . . .

Organizations

If you would like to find out more about Central America or about human rights abuse in some of its countries, the organizations listed below can provide you with more information. When you write, be sure to be specific about what you want to know, and always include your name, age, and mailing address.

Americas Watch
485 Fifth Avenue
New York, NY 10017

Amnesty International
322 Eighth Avenue
New York, NY 10001

Children's Urgent Action Network
P. O. Box 1270
Nederland, CO 80466

Embassy of Costa Rica
1825 Connecticut Avenue NW
Suite 211
Washington DC 20009

Organization of American States (OAS)
Seventeenth Street and Constitution
   Avenue NW
Washington DC 20006

The Resource Center
P. O. Box 4506
Albuquerque, NM 87196

Commission for the Defense of Human
   Rights in Central America
Paseo de los Estudiantes
Apartado 189
San Jose, Costa Rica

Books and Articles

About Oscar Arias Sánchez —

"Arias: Whom Can He Trust?" *New York Times Magazine.* January 10, 1988
"More Than a Peacemaker," *Commonweal.* December 4, 1987
Nobel Costa Rica. Seth Rolbein (St. Martins Press)

About Costa Rica —

"The Central America Peace Plan," *Current History.* December 1987
The Costa Ricans. Richard Biesanz (Prentice-Hall)
Costa Rica: Nature, Prosperity, and Peace on the Rich Coast. Allen M. Young
   (Interamerican Research Corp.)

About Central America —

"Will the Arias Peace Plan Work?" *World Press Review.* October 1987
"Ortega: Can He Be Trusted?" *New York Times Magazine.* January 10, 1988
Central America, A Nation Divided. Ralph L. Woodward, Jr. (Oxford)
Conflict in Central America. Helen Schooley (St. James Press)
The Central American Fact Book. Tom Barry and Deb Preusch (Grove)

Glossary

amnesty
> A pardon for people accused of crimes and offenses, thereby freeing them from punishment. All political prisoners in Central America were to receive amnesty as part of the Arias peace plan.

aristocracy
> The highest social and economic class. Because Oscar Arias was born to one of Costa Rica's wealthy coffee-growing families, he is a member of the aristocracy.

campesino
> A Spanish term meaning "peasant." The majority of Central Americans are campesinos who live and work on farms.

cease-fire
> An agreement between warring groups or nations to stop fighting temporarily.

Central Intelligence Agency (CIA)
> An organization of the United States government that secretly gathers information about other nations and conducts secret military operations to promote U.S. political and economic interests.

civil war
> A war fought between political or religious groups within one country. The left-wing guerrillas in El Salvador are fighting a civil war with the right-wing rulers in the attempt to gain control of the country.

colón
> The Costa Rican unit of money, named after Cristobál Colón (Christopher Columbus).

communism
> A social system where the government controls all economic and political activities, and wealth is evenly distributed. There is no private ownership of property in a purely communist system.

contras
> A guerrilla army, widely accused of terrorism, made up of enemies of the Sandinistas, including former National Guardsmen of the Somoza government.

coup d'etat
> The forceful removal of any governing body or leader, usually by military means. In 1936, Anastasio Somoza led a coup d'etat against President Juan Bautista Sacasa, establishing a dictatorship that would rule Nicaragua for the next forty-three years.

dictator
> An absolute ruler who is not answerable to any authority but his or her own. Often, dictators are not elected by democratic process but assume power by using military force or political guile.

Escuadrones de Muerte
> The Spanish term for "Death Squads," which are armed groups organized by the Salvadoran, Guatemalan, and Honduran governments to kill their political

opponents and any civilian resistors. Since 1979, death squads in Central America have killed at least 60,000 people.

Esquipulas II Accords

The formal name for the Central America Peace Plan signed by the presidents of Costa Rica, El Salvador, Honduras, Guatemala, and Nicaragua on August 7, 1987, in Esquipulas, Guatemala.

Farabundo Martí National Liberation Front (FMLN)

A conglomeration of five left-wing rebel groups in El Salvador named for Farabundo Martí, a revolutionary leader.

finca

The Spanish term for "farm" or "ranch."

guerrilla

The Spanish term for "warrior," usually referring to a fighter who is not in the regular army, but who is a member of a secret resistance group. The contras and the FMLN are guerrilla organizations fighting against their governments.

human rights

The basic rights to which every human being is entitled, without regard to race, religion, nationality, sex, age, or political beliefs. Human rights include equal access to food, clothing, shelter, and education. As well, privacy, freedom from torture and murder, freedom of speech and religious worship, the right to be treated as equals under the law, and the right to vote are also human rights.

intellectual

Someone of high intelligence who is rational, learned, and thoughtful.

isthmus

A narrow strip of land connecting two larger masses of land. Central America is an isthmus connecting North and South America.

junta

The Spanish term for "council." Military juntas are common ruling bodies during a revolution.

left-wing

A term describing liberal, progressive, or radical political beliefs. Left wing supporters tend to value political change in the name of the greater freedom or well-being of the common people.

matanza

The Spanish term for "massacre."

National Liberation Party (PLN)

The political party that established democracy and the constitution in Costa Rica , and which has been the majority party for many years. Oscar Arias is a member of the PLN, as was his mentor, José Figueres.

negotiation

Discussions between people or groups that are held in the hope that they will lead to a mutually satisfying agreement. Oscar Arias negotiated with the presidents of four other Central American countries until they agreed to a peace plan.

Nicaraguan Opposition Union (UNO)
A group of Nicaraguan political parties that got together to oppose the Sandinistas in 1989. In 1990, Violeta Chamorro, the UNO candidate, was elected president of Nicaragua.

neutrality
Not taking sides in any conflict. Costa Rica and Switzerland are neutral countries who take no part in the wars of their neighbors.

Nobel Peace Prize
The annual prize awarded by the Nobel Committee in Oslo, Norway, to the person who has shown the greatest dedication to peace in the world. Oscar Arias won the Nobel Peace Prize in 1987 for promoting peace in Central America.

oligarchy
A system of government where a few self-appointed individuals rule. In the early 1900s, El Salvador was ruled by an oligarchy of fourteen families.

PhD
The Doctor of Philosophy degree, awarded to a person who completes additional years of education beyond college. Oscar Arias has a PhD in Political Economy which he earned at the University of Sussex in England.

politics
The methods of managing government, or a philosophy of how government should be run; sometimes it is called "political science."

refugee
A person who flees from one place to another to escape danger or persecution. Thousands of refugees have fled Central America in search of safety and peace.

repression
To forcefully prevent someone from speaking or taking action. The government's repression in El Salvador is so harsh that many citizens are afraid to speak their minds for fear of being killed by a death squad.

revolution
To overthrow the government by force. The Sandinistas led the revolution that removed the Somoza dictators from power.

right-wing
A term describing conservative political beliefs. Right-wing supporters value social conformity and adherence to traditional roles, and favor a free market economy and uncontrolled property ownership.

Sandinista Front for National Liberation (FSLN)
The Nicaraguan political party named after rebel leader Augusto César Sandino, who became the martyr of modern Nicaragua history after he was murdered by members of Anastasio Somoza's National Guard. The Sandinistas, as members of the party are known, overthrew the Somoza dictatorship in the 1979 revolution.

terrorism
Illegal acts of violence committed against military or civilian targets to achieve political ends. Death squads engage in terrorism when they kill people who oppose the government.

Chronology

1502   Christopher Columbus lands on the beaches of Costa Rica on his fourth voyage to the west.

1564   Looking for gold, Don Juan Vasquez de Coronado settles first Spanish colony in Costa Rica.

1821   Costa Rica joins Guatemala, El Salvador, Honduras, and Nicaragua in declaring independence from Spain.

1850   Coffee becomes Costa Rica's main export.

1856   Costa Rica regains its independence from an American invader named William Walker, who had briefly conquered and ruled.

1912   The U.S. Marines occupy Nicaragua to help the Conservative Party overthrow the government.

1926   Augusto César Sandino organizes an army of Nicaraguan peasants to resist U.S. occupation.

1933   Sandino's army is victorious. Before leaving Nicaragua, the marines form a National Guard led by Anastasio Somoza.

1934   Sandino is assassinated by Somoza's National Guard.

1936   Somoza becomes the military dictator of Nicaragua.

1941   **September 13** — Oscar Arias Sánchez is born in Heredia, Costa Rica.

1942   Costa Rica sinks deeply into debt due to the expenses of running the army and building the Pan American Highway.

1945   President Calderón of Costa Rica sets up a workers' bill of rights. The country sinks farther into debt.

1948   **April** — President Teodoro Picado of Costa Rica declares the presidential election null and void. José Figueres Ferrer wages civil war to restore democracy and becomes temporary president.
Twenty-one Central, North, and South American countries form the Organization of American States (OAS) to promote peace and security. The group includes Costa Rica, El Salvador, Guatemala, Honduras, and Nicaragua.

1949   Figueres drafts a new constitution for Costa Rica and abolishes the army.

1951   Figueres founds the National Liberation Party (PLN).

1956   Anastasio Somoza is assassinated. His son, Luis Somoza Debayle, becomes dictator.

1961	Arias wins an essay competition held by *La Nacion* newspaper. The Sandinista Front for National Liberation (FSLN) forms and begins to wage guerrilla warfare against the Somoza government.
1961-1975	Over 350,000 Salvadoran campesinos flee their country because of the unbearable conditions there.
1962	Arias attends the University of Costa Rica in San José. He becomes a member of the National Liberation Party (PLN).
1964	Arias meets José Figueres Ferrer and becomes his protégé.
1965-1966	Arias works on the presidential election campaign of a PLN candidate.
1966	Right-wing death squads emerge in Guatemala.
1967	Luis Somoza Debayle dies. His brother, Anastasio Somoza Debayle, becomes dictator. Arias graduates from the university. He goes to England, where he studies at the University of Essex and London School of Economics.
1969-1972	Arias returns to Costa Rica and becomes a professor at the University of Costa Rica.
1970	Arias publishes *Pressure Groups in Costa Rica*, his first book. It wins the National Essay Prize. **May** — José Figueres is elected president and appoints Arias as his economic adviser.
1972-1977	**August** — Figueres appoints Arias as the minister of national planning and political economy.
1973	Arias marries Margarita Penón Góngora.
1974	Arias' *Who Governs Costa Rica?* is published.
1975	**August**— Arias is elected the PLN's international secretary.
1976	**November** — Arias oversees the building of the Plaza de Cultura in San José.
1977	Arias holds a symposium to discuss the future of Costa Rica. He publishes the reports in a book entitled *Costa Rica in the Year 2000*.
1978	**February** — Arias is elected to the national legislative assembly as a representative of his home district, Heredia.
1979	**July 19** — The Sandinistas overthrow the Somoza government. **September**— Somoza's National Guard re-forms into the rebel contra army. The contras begin receiving weapons and training from the United States. Arias is elected general secretary of the PLN, the party's highest post.
1980	**March** — El Salvador's death squads kill Archbishop Oscar Romero. The first U.S. military trainers arrive in Honduras. **October** — Left-wing guerillas in El Salvador found the Farabundo Martí

National Liberation Front (FMLN), a rebel army, and launch a civil war against the government.

December — Four U.S. nuns are killed by Salvadoran death squads. U.S. Aid to El Salvador is halted temporarily.

José Napoleón Duarte is inaugurated as president of El Salvador.

1981   Arias helps Luis Alberto Monge, a PLN candidate, to run for president. Monge is elected in February of 1982.

U.S. aid to El Salvador's government resumes.

1983   Arias is re-elected as general secretary of the PLN.

1984   **January** — Arias seeks his party's nomination for the presidency.

The Sandinistas hold elections in Nicaragua. Daniel Ortega Saavedra is elected president and forms close ties with the Soviet Union.

U.S. President Ronald Reagan claims the election was rigged.

June — José Napoleón Duarte is re-elected as president of El Salvador.

1985   Thousands of contras move to Costa Rica.

1986   **January 14** — Vinicio Cerezo Arévalo is inaugurated as president of Guatemala.

José Azcona Hoyo is inaugurated as president of Honduras.

February — Arias is elected president of Costa Rica.

May 8 — Arias is inaugurated as Costa Rica's forty-seventh president. He is the youngest person to hold this office.

May 24-25 — Arias meets with the presidents of Nicaragua, El Salvador, Guatemala, and Honduras to propose a peace plan for Central America.

November — Arias orders all contras to leave Costa Rica. The U.S. withholds over $80 million in aid in retaliation.

1987   **February 17** — Arias negotiates his peace plan with the presidents of El Salvador, Guatemala, and Honduras. The plan calls for democratic elections and the ending of all military aid from outside countries.

August 7 — The five Central American presidents sign the "Esquipulas II" peace plan in Esquipulas, Guatemala.

October 13 — Oscar Arias is awarded the Nobel Peace Prize.

December 1 — Arias proclaims this day a national holiday to celebrate Costa Rica's abolition of the army. José Figueres is honored.

1988   **February 13** — The five treaty signers meet in Costa Rica to discuss the progress of the peace plan. Daniel Ortega agrees to hold democratic elections in one year and abide by the results.

1990   **January** — Oscar Arias receives an approval rating of 80% from the Costa Rican people.

February 4 — Rafael Calderón, Jr. is elected the next president of Costa Rica and is openly critical of the Arias peace plan.

President José Napoleón Duarte of El Salvador dies. Alfredo Cristiani is elected to replace him. Cristiani agrees to negotiate with the left-wing rebels.

February 26 — Democratic elections are held in Nicaragua.

Violeta Chamorro of the Nicaraguan Opposition Union (UNO) defeats Daniel Ortega and is elected president.

April 19 — The contras and Sandinistas agree to a permanent cease-fire. Chamorro is sworn in as president of Nicaragua.

April 25 — Violeta Chamorro is inaugurated as president of Nicaragua.

May 5 — Oscar Arias leaves the office of president of Costa Rica.

Index